AUTHOR
DRIVER, C.

CLASS
E02

TITLE
Bolton

Sutton Publishing Limited
Phoenix Mill · Thrupp · Stroud
Gloucestershire · GL5 2BU

First published 1999

Copyright © Chris Driver, 1999

British Library Cataloguing in Publication Data
A catalogue record for this book is available from the
British Library.

ISBN 0-7509-0974-9

Typeset in 10.5/13.5 Photina.
Typesetting and origination by
Sutton Publishing Limited.
Printed in Great Britain by
Redwood Books,Ltd., Trowbridge.

Rivington Hall Barn before Leverhulme restored and extended it by adding a toilet block, tearoom and porch. The medieval cruck construction barn is still standing and is one of the most popular venues for shows, fairs, dances and concerts. It is a mecca for motorcyclists who come from miles around every Sunday – in fine weather.

CONTENTS

The Bolton area relief map, 1934. This large-scale map illustrates the topography of Bolton and the area up to 10 miles around it. It shows especially well the heights of Winter Hill (1,456 ft) and the surrounding moors, which at this time were without the now familiar plantations of conifers planted over a decade later. Where Bolton now stands the melting ice of the later Ice Age formed a great lake extending far to the south. Into this flowed what was to become the River Croal, bringing stones, pebbles, mud and sand, and depositing it along with crushed rocks and soil. These are still under Bolton to a depth of over 100 ft in places: it is described as boulder clay. This map used to be on display in Bolton Museum.

INTRODUCTION & ACKNOWLEDGEMENTS

This book is not a history of the Bolton area. We are fortunate in our town to have a treasure house of local information in our archives and local history sections in the main library and the local history section of the museum. All are staffed by experts in their field and anyone wishing to delve deeper into our town's history should seek advice there. Many of the pictures included here could be researched for weeks, and often are by enthusiasts of buses, trains, trams, cars, and so on, or perhaps just for nostalgic reasons.

The book is more a collection of snapshots of life over the last hundred years. Snapshots like this are seldom taken now except for our local newspaper, the *Bolton Evening News*. In these days when everyone has a compact camera it is rare for people to use them to record everyday life. I would like to think that in 2099 there will be records of everyday life in Bolton for people to look at and enjoy.

My sincere thanks to my wife Janet for help and encouragement.

Thanks to Paula Ashworth for everything.

Thanks also to Mike Dudley.

For a wealth of received information I must thank my good friend James Pilkington, landlord of probably the finest public house in Lancashire.

Mention also must be made of my ex-colleagues and good friends Kevin Campbell, Barry Mills and Sharron, Angela Thomas and especially Rick Bradbury.

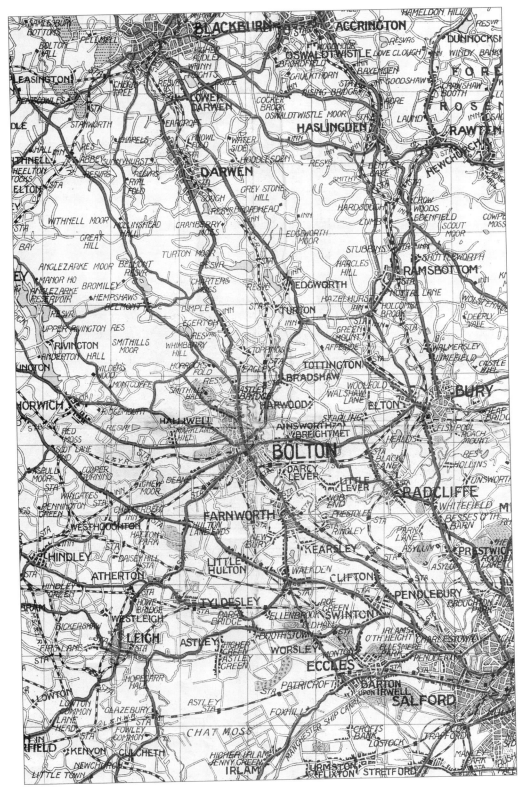

Bolton and surrounding area.

CHAPTER ONE

TOWN CENTRE

Churchgate, from a painting by George Bury, 1815. St Peter's parish church was possibly the fourth church sinc
Saxon times to have occupied the site. No individual properties can be identified except perhaps Walsh's Pasti
Shop, second left, but the picture gives an idea of the pleasing lines and symmetry of Churchgate.

Opposite, above: The old parish church prior to demolition in 1866, before the rails were laid for the trucks to carr
away the debris. There are various and confusing dates for photographs of the medieval church and demolition
one usually authoritative work states that 'the Bolton Parish Church of St Peter was demolished in 1866' (C.H
Saxelby, *Bolton Survey*, 1953).

Samuel Crompton's tomb is shown in fine condition in this view, which was published in December 1893 b
Thomas Bromley, 32 Bradshawgate and Fold Street, Bolton, and printed in Austria.

Below: The medieval St Peter's Church from the east, looking towards Churchgate. The fine decorated tracery c
the east window can still be seen. The building was demolished for two reasons. The main one was that it wa
sliding downhill into Churchbank and the River Croal, and was heavily buttressed on the north side; the othe
was that since the eighteenth century, because of the growing population of the town, the church had become to
small for the congregation.

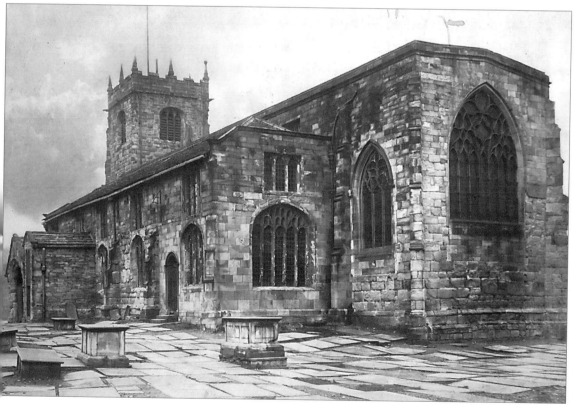

The west doorway of the medieval St Peter's Church during demolition, probably 1866. Repair had become impossible. Here is the old clock face which for many years looked down Churchgate, accompanied by undoubtedly the foreman-in-charge with a young worker behind in the roofless interior. Fragments of stained glass lie to the right of the doorway.

The photograph was taken by Reuben Mitchell and was sold in stereoscopic card form.

The Church Institute, *c.* 1868. The photograph was taken during demolition of the old parish church (to the left), while the old Grammar School can be seen on the right.

The Church Institute. Although there is still an Institute Street near the parish church there is no trace of the building, which opened in 1855 as the Bolton Church of England Educational Institution. In June 1946 it became Canon Slade Grammar School to honour the Vicar of Bolton from 1817 to 1856, Canon Slade. The school itself moved to Bradshaw in January 1956. In 1957–8 it was used to store furniture by Battersbys' (Bolton) Limited and later as an annexe for Bolton Technical College. The building was demolished in 1969, and the meeting house of Bolton's Religious Society of Friends is now on the site.

Inside the old Bolton Grammar School, 1880. Thomas Parkinson, the usher who took over after the last headmaster had left, is on the left. The school was built during Cromwell's Government with money from the will of Robert Lever from Darcy Lever, who was a merchant in London. The Grammar School, which was founded in 1524, moved to this building in 1658. The school was demolished in 1899 and the new building on the site is the Parish Hall opened in 1976.

Churchgate, looking east towards the parish church and through a battlemented arch decked with flags and bunting for Queen Victoria's Golden Jubilee, 1887. To the right is the Star Inn which replaced the notorious Star Theatre of Varieties, one of the town's moral blackspots in the early years of the Queen's reign. Next was the Theatre Royal, whose scenery builders and proprietor Mr Ellison were responsible for the wooden arch. A grand turn-out of cabs and cabbies is ready for a special Jubilee event. The banner to the left is that of the Sons of Isaac Walton and that to the right belongs to the Hearts of Oak Lodge.

Churchgate, 1897. The Swan Hotel is decorated in fine style for Queen Victoria's Diamond Jubilee. The licensee and his wife, Mr and Mrs Henry Greenwood, are at the door. It is possible that there was a Swan here before 1600, and the engravings of the execution of the Earl of Derby in 1651 show the building. The buildings photographed were of 1845, and were extended and altered in 1930 and again in 1984–5.

A peculiar local form of hoaxing strangers is associated with the Swan. A local man with a wooden leg would bet unwitting strangers to match the time he could keep his leg in a tub of boiling water. It was named trotting, and the nickname for a Boltonian is also a 'trotter', although at least three other explanations for the nickname exist.

Churchgate, c. 1890. This scene is now almost unrecognisable, but a useful reference point is the alley or ginnel to Gaskell Court and 'Mrs Davis's Good Lodgings'. No. 11 was James Booth's music shop and next door at No. 13 was the Golden Lion (or t'Brass Cat), which from 1772 to 1778 was known as the Bear's Paw and from 1779 to 1806 as the Crown and Thistle. It was doubled in size in 1966. The little shop to the far right at No. 15 was W. Handy's; he had a barber's business here from 1885 to 1895 but the little shop had a more famous tenant, also a barber and wigmaker, from 1785/6 to 1796: Richard Arkwright. He invented a machine, the water frame, which was soon adopted by Bolton cotton spinners. The building was demolished in 1910 but a plaque on the building that replaced it commemorates Arkwright. It is now Booth's music shop.

The Swan Hotel, Churchgate, with flags and bunting ready for the Diamond Jubilee celebrations in 1897. Over the entrance on the balcony is a magnificent lifesize gilded model of Victoria. The Swan dates back to the late seventeenth century and in 1790 the mail coach used to leave here for Manchester. The building in the centre of the road is a cabmen's shelter, erected in about 1870 but removed early in the twentieth century. The drinking fountain was removed during the drive for scrap metal during the Second World War.

Churchgate, looking east from the market cross to the parish church. A market cross has been on this site since the thirteenth century, set up (as was usual) close to a parish church to symbolise the centre of town life and to mark the market-place. In 1748 the famous preacher John Wesley preached on the steps of a previous cross – and was stoned by the crowd. That cross was moved in 1786 and is now in the grounds of Bolton School. The present cross dates from 29 November 1909.

The old parish church vicarage, from the parish church gates, looking north, 1928. The building to the left of the man who is standing in what Bolton people call a ginnel was Mrs Harley's boarding house, home to theatrical people when they were performing at the Churchgate theatres. It later became offices for a variety of businesses, including the Bolton Lead Works, the sign for which is over another ginnel to the left. The block of buildings to the left was demolished to make way for Fletcher's Church House Garage.

Churchgate, but captioned Park Street, with some wonderful artistic additions to the parish church to turn it into a grand cathedral, very early 1900s. This fascinating card was printed in Germany.

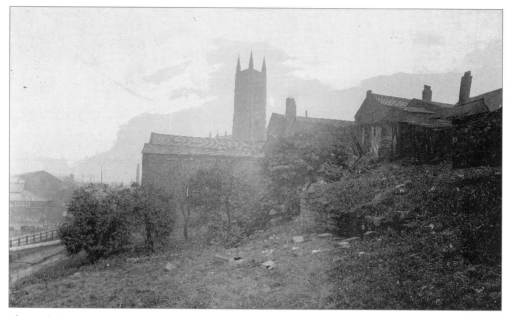

The cock-fighting pit, Antelope Court, *c. 1927.* This picture shows the outline of the arena, which was about 2 ft below ground level, while the higher walled slopes were for spectators. Just below the parish church was John Crook's safe works with Bolton Lead Works to the right. To the extreme right is the Boars Head public house, now the Varsity.

Antelope Court, *c. 1927.* In the centre of the view is the edge of the cock-fighting pit with the River Croal beyond and below. Cock fighting was made illegal in Bolton in 1843, but this site and others were used a lot later than that.

Churchgate from Churchbank, 1955–60. This photograph shows the imposing bulk of the Grand Theatre and the Legs of Man Hotel. Behind the lamp on the right was originally the Imperial Hotel, previously known as the Rising Sun, at 5 Churchbank. It closed in 1934 with the transfer of the licence to the King's Arms, Chorley Old Road. It was well known as temporary lodgings for acts at the Theatre Royal and the Grand but was the Regent Film Library by the late 1950s. To the extreme right is Tempest and O'Hara, wholesale clothiers and manufacturers.

Brown Street and Well Street, from the north side of the parish church tower, 1964. This is not an old photograph, but much has changed in this area just north of the River Croal, which is in the foreground. Most of the land to the centre right is now used for car parking and to the left, over what was Whitehurst's Corn Mill, is now a multi-storey car park. In the top right-hand corner were the Co-op Dairy and Moscrops Lion Oil Works, once destined to become an industrial museum but later sold to become a nightclub. Almost all of this area has been demolished (September 1999) to form a car park.

Church Wharf, 1965. This was one end of the Bolton, Bury and Manchester Canal, begun in 1790. The wharf (at the very bottom right) was used by barges until 1950. The three-storey Georgian building in the centre is the Bull and Wharf Hotel, built to serve what became a busy port and demolished in 1966 in preparation for St Peter's Way, which has now replaced almost the whole of the right of the picture. The church is St John's, the cooling tower is Back o' th' Bank power station, and in the lower left-hand corner is 'Knacker' Brown's slaughterhouse.

Bradshawgate, 1902. This photograph was probably taken just before the Volunteer Inn, to the right, was renamed the Empire. The Empire closed in 1905 and was demolished to make way for the widening of Bradshawgate to the dimensions of today. To the extreme right of the Volunteer is probably Mr Whittaker, who kept a café there until the whole block was demolished. No. 50 Bradshawgate to the left is Ramsden's music shop, one of many in the town centre selling new and secondhand instruments. It had a loan facility for weekend buskers. Virtually everything in this shot is now demolished, again to facilitate parking.

The Bradshawgate corner of Nelson Square, *c.* 1902. Just before this date the electric tram had begun to run down Deansgate. The small hotel on the corner was the Pack Horse Hotel, which was demolished in 1904 to make way for the grand new Pack Horse Hotel of 1906. This is now one of the largest hotels in Bolton. Next door was Aubrey Franks, opticians and photographic equipment dealers, which was demolished at the same time and moved to 90 Bradshawgate, near the Balmoral Hotel. One of Bolton's early cinemas, the Paragon, was built next door to the Pack Horse and opened in 1914. It was demolished in January 1935 to make way for the Bradshawgate Arcade.

A group of workmen, possibly floorlayers, outside the newly completed Pack Horse Hotel, Bradshawgate, Nelson Square, 1904. While this imposing structure was being built the licence continued for eighteen months in a wooden hut at the back. The Pack Horse continued to expand eastwards, with the acquisition and demolition of the Reform Club (by this time the Lever's Arms Hotel) in Bowkers Row in 1949.

A busy view of Nelson Square from Bradshawgate, looking west, 1900. To the extreme left is the Prudential building of 1898 with Wales' tobacconist and hairdresser next door. In the centre of the block at Nos 20–24 is Scholes & Scholes, merchant tailors, who occupied this popular square for over sixty years before moving to other premises: these buildings are the only ones remaining today. Further up the square were various premises used as offices by accountants and surveyors. At No. 10 were the offices of Richard Hough, makers of calender bowls for industry, with their works at the rear (the chimney is Hough's). At the head of the square is the Infirmary, built in 1827 and taken over in 1883 by the Education Department. The building was demolished in 1972 to make way for Provincial House, built in 1974. In the centre is the statue of Samuel Crompton, dating from 1862.

Nelson Square, c. 1900. To the left are the former Education Offices, demolished in 1972, which occupied what was previously the Bolton Infirmary, which had only seven beds. For the peace and quiet of the patients the whole of the square was paved in wooden blocks, which when taken up were bought by Roberts Lead Works, Windley Street. The Levers Arms, middle left, known as the Cock and Trumpet, was demolished in 1949 and the Pack Horse Hotel was extended on the site in 1952. Next to that was the Nelson Hairdressing Salon. The box in front of the Samuel Crompton monument was for collecting books, newspapers and so on for the use of the sick and infirm inmates of the Bolton Union Workhouse.

Nelson Square twenty years on, 29 July 1920. The Duke of York is at the Artillery War Memorial; he was in Bolton visiting the Royal Lancashire Agricultural Show held at Lostock. Later, in 1954, General M.W. Dewry unveiled a plaque on the memorial to commemorate 151 men of the Bolton Artillery killed during the Second World War. The gardens are still a popular spot on a sunny day.

The Samuel Crompton Centenary, Nelson Square, 1927. The Mayor and other dignitaries laid floral tributes at Samuel Crompton's monument. The centenary was attended by people from around the world connected with the cotton trade. The statue cost over £2,000, raised by subscriptions from the public, and was unveiled in 1862 – thirty-two years after Crompton died in poverty after giving his invention, Crompton's Mule, to the world. Crompton's only surviving son, John, was brought out of Bolton Workhouse for the unveiling, and taken straight back when the junketings and jollifications began. There is a fine but plain tomb for Samuel Crompton in St Peter's churchyard.

Bradshawgate, 1936. Tram H to Doffcocker is just passing Yates Wine Lodge. The trams had not long to run, and many services including this one were replaced by motor buses in 1939. Next to Yates was Ship Gates, which took its name from the Ship Inn which fronted on to Bradshawgate. In 1890 Yates Ltd bought the Bull's Head adjoining the Ship Inn and registered it as their fifth Wine Lodge in the country. The terracotta building of 1906 is still there today. Shipgates was closed as a thoroughfare after a court case of 1975, and Fold Street to the left was closed for the Arndale precinct, making it now the shortest street in Bolton. Until 1969 it linked Bradshawgate to Acresfield.

Longton's Pie Shop, Bradshawgate, July 1921. The lorry is being loaded with 5,325 meat pies for the Queen Street Mission annual Poor Children's Outing to Rivington. Edward Longton is on the lorry in a bowler hat. Next door to the pie shop is the Oddfellows Arms, owned originally by Seed's then Magee Marshall and closed by them in 1938. The premises were last used by Marie's Hairdressers until 1959, and demolished in 1962 to become Metrolands House.

The Fleece Hotel, Bradshawgate. A Fleece Inn stood here from the early nineteenth century, but was demolished during the road-widening scheme in 1907. The new Fleece Hotel was a splendid terracotta building put up some time after 1907, and featured these splendid gas lamps. Like many Bolton hotels it suffered from refurbishment; from 1972 to 1983 it was The Gaiety and was renamed Maxim's in July 1983. Just visible to the right is Kendall's rainwear premises.

Fold Street at the junction with Bradshawgate. Now the shortest street in town, prior to its closure in 1969 Fold Street was very busy and used by a great variety of professions and trades. There were architects, solicitors, accountants and auctioneers mixed with Chez Aristotle's restaurant and the Silver Grill, who rubbed shoulders with the City Toilet Saloon (hairdressers). The street may once have been named Lever Street but was renamed in honour of Parson Folds (1755–1820), local character and lecturer (giver of religious instruction) of Bolton parish church, in July 1806. Franks Yard to the extreme left is seen here as a car park; Frank's identity is unknown.

Deansgate, *c*. 1880. This was the Bank of Bolton, known as the Cotton Bank because all its directors were cotton magnates. The building doubled in size with the demolition of the Cross Axes public house early in 1900, and Cross Axe Entry became Woods Court. In 1935 it became the District Bank and later the National Westminster. There are now eight stone heads over the present bank: it is not known who they represent.

Deansgate, looking west, decked out with flags and decorations for the celebrations of Queen Victoria's Golden Jubilee, 1887. Next to Monk Bros, watchmakers and jewellers, on the extreme right can just be seen the first Whiteheads shop in Bolton at the Crown Street junction, with further down the Old Three Crowns, the Bank of Bolton and just visible the turret of Williams Deacons Bank.

Looking east down Deansgate towards Churchgate and the parish church, very soon after the arrival in Bolton of electric trams in 1900. Prominent to the near right behind the magnificent gas lamp was the Manchester and County Bank, and left of centre was Constantine Brothers, silk merchants and drapers. The building which stood from 1854 was known as Britannia House because of the huge figure of Britannia which dominated the Deansgate skyline until it was dismantled and burnt in September 1942. Woolworth's is now on the site.

Joiners Arms, 15a Deansgate, 1900. A popular town centre hostelry for over a century, this pub used to be nick-named Bathe's Vaults but was later referred to as t'Big Tug until closure in 1958. This building was replaced by the present three-storey one, but the Joiners Arms remained – with the main bar at the rear of the building. The Danish Dairy Co. later became the Maypole Dairy Co., and down the ginnel (which is still there) was Kemball Bros Co., tea and coffee merchants.

Deansgate and Bradshawgate Corner, 1905. This area was a popular meeting place known as Hope's Corner, the firm of Hope Brothers (The Smart Outfitting Company) giving it its name. Hope's building was taken over by the Swan Hotel; the present building dates back to about 1845, but a Swan stood here in the early seventeenth century. The Swan was extended and altered in 1930–1 and again in 1984–5. Like many of these town centre junction postcards it features a 'bobby' on point duty with little or no traffic.

Spring Gardens and Howell Croft, from Deansgate looking south, 1910. In the centre is the aptly named Junction Inn, closed in 1908 as part of the slum clearance programme. The two closer chimneys are Blackhorse Mill, built in 1849 by Rothwell & Kitts and demolished in 1995, and behind are those of Union Foundry, later the Bessemer Steel Works, demolished in 1927.

Deansgate looking east, from the Knowsley Street junction, 1928. The Paragon Dress House of T. Bullough & Co. on the corner moved to Knowsley Street shortly after this picture was taken. Next door to the Paragon, advertising Swan pens and inks, was George Winterburn's newsagents. On the left, with the usual crop of travel posters, was the office of Thomas Cook & Sons Ltd, travel agents. Next door to Cook's was a 'bazaar' run by Marks & Spencer Ltd, known at the time as 'the penny store'.

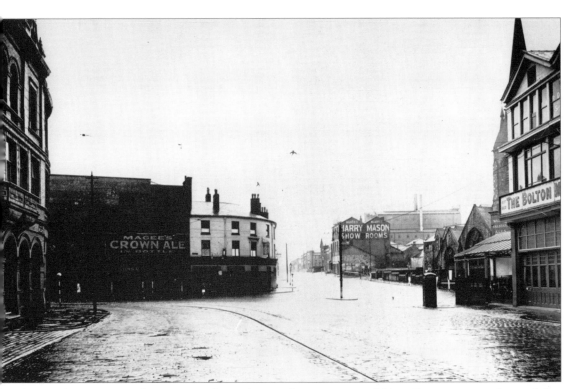

Marsden Road, Deansgate. The junction of Marsden Road, Deansgate and Moor Lane on a wet, deserted day, 1940. To the extreme left is the main fire station, still in use then. Across the road to the left is Deansgate Warehouse, which until the 1920s was served by a branch railway line of the LNWR company which ran through and across three main town centre streets. It was demolished in 1963. Next door is the White Lion and to the right Harry Mason's showrooms for household goods. Next to the right and just visible are the Sunday Schools and St Paul's Church. Across Spa Road is the Gypsies Tent public house and the Bolton Motor Co., not presently motorcars but motorcycles and occupied by ESB.

The Hippodrome, Deansgate, October 1968. Bolton's earliest theatre was the Old Theatre in Acres Field, thought to date from the early eighteenth century and lasting until the late 1860s. The Hippodrome was an unusually designed building of about 1908; it became a cinema in 1923 but reverted to a 'rep' theatre from 1940 until 1961, when closure meant the end of professional permanent theatre in Bolton. The establishment of the excellent Octagon Theatre in November 1967 marked a welcome return, with the opening of one-time Boltonian Bill Naughton's play *Annie and Fanny*. The Hippodrome's site is now for sale, but was previously Deansgate Health Centre.

The Kings Arms, Deansgate, *c.* 1909. Kings Heads and Arms are not plentiful in the Bolton area perhaps because of the Civil War, but this one was a popular hostelry from the very early 1800s until closure in 1962. This picture shows the then landlady Elizabeth Ashworth, who took over on the death of her husband Henry sometime between 1908 and 1910. It was later used as a religious bookshop and from 1974 to 1980 was named Chapter and Verse; it became Sweetens bookshop in 1980.

Deansgate and Ridgway Gates, early 1960. Podmore's seeds and garden shop (far left) was here from the 1920s to the 1970s. The Kings Arms closed in 1962, while next door was Edward Crook, fish and game dealer since 1933. The shop was probably altered in 1907 to match the new Tudor-style shop of Whitakers across the road. The Dolcis shoe shop with original sash windows was occupied by them from the 1930s until the late 1960s.

The Market Hall. In the 1850s the Town Council, led by T.L. Rushton, cleared slums and old buildings between Deansgate and the River Croal to build a covered market and also carry Knowsley Street on a grand stone viaduct over the river. The Market Hall, which cost around £100,000, opened in time for Christmas 1855, followed ten years later by the Fish Market. The interior layout (below in about 1900) lasted until it was replaced by blocks of stalls 'of modern design' in 1938. The balcony, which ran the full length of the building, used to have stalls selling livestock and pets, from ducks and geese to rabbits. Many stallholders moved to the new Ashburner Street market in 1932, which itself was modernised in 1996.

The opening of Victoria Hall, Knowsley Street, 1900, probably taken from the Market Hall balcony.
As well as being the home of Methodism in Bolton, this fine building is used for concerts and recitals.

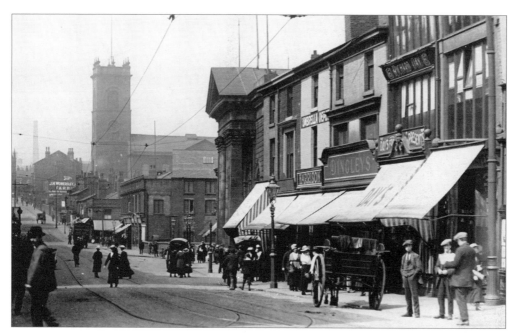

Knowsley Street, looking north towards the Market Hall and St George's Church, *c.* 1920. The distant chimney of Barlow and Jones' Albert Mill is just visible. To the right is Richard Day's family leather goods shop and next door is Dingleys, fruiterer and florist; next is Harrison's umbrella shop. On the corner with Corporation Street is Bon Marché, fancy drapers and milliners.

Knowsley Street, 1928. This photograph was probably taken in the early morning as very few people can be seen, and there is no traffic for the policeman to direct. This was usually a very busy junction and almost all trams coming in or out of town would cross here. Up to 1928 the site had a permanent 'points boy' who had to switch the tracks by hand. This system was replaced by a box with levers to do the job situated in a safer pavement site, and in 1931 the whole thing became automatic. The wood and glass hut to the right was the Corporation Tramways waiting room, removed in 1928.

Knowsley Street/Bark Street corner, 1972. The photograph was taken before the Flax Mill chimney w
demolished to make way for the Bark Street development scheme. Flax or Bark Street Mills dated back to abo
1820, when Brooks and Smith spun flax. Knowsley Street was widened after the 1850 Bolton Improvement A
on land owned by the Earls of Derby. As Derby Street had already been named this thoroughfare was named aft
the ancient seat of the Derbys, near Liverpool.

Sir Benjamin Dobson, Mayor of
Bolton, on the Town Hall steps,
1897. The Town Hall was
decorated with wreaths and
bunting for the Diamond Jubilee (
Queen Victoria; the rope behind
the assembled group held huge
lanterns which were hoisted up a
night. For some reason the Jubilee
was not celebrated in the town
with as much enthusiasm as the
1887 Jubilee, when the entire
town almost vanished under flags
banners and triumphal arches,
although there was a 'Patriotic
Concert' in Queen's Park. This ca
was produced by J. Hinchcliffe of
17 Blackbank Street, and was
widely copied.

Bolton Corporation Fire Station, 1899. The service was removed to Marsden Road later in 1899 after occupying this site for twenty-eight years. W.H. Houghton's boot and shoe shop had its frontage on Newport Street and the back (seen here) on Coronation Street. The exact location today would be the corner of the Octagon car park behind what was for years the Wheatsheaf public house. The old wholesale fruit and vegetable market was just behind the photographer.

Bolton as it might have been if Mr W.H. Lever (later Lord Leverhulme) had been allowed to plan it. He engaged the architect Thomas Mawson to replan the streets of the town as wide, sweeping boulevards; the most impressive swept from the Town Hall to an almost acropolis-like museum in Queen's Park. This vision of 1910 came to nothing.

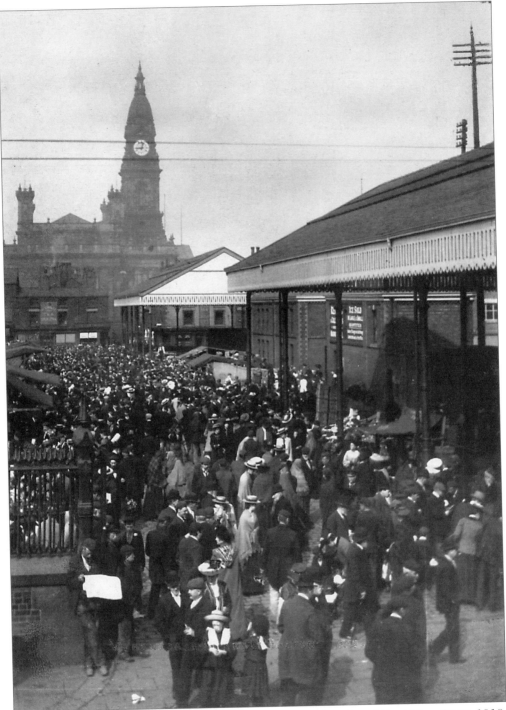

A busy Saturday scene at Ashburner Street Market, from the direction of Great Moor Street, 1910. Crowds of shoppers are buying their fruit and vegetables for the week. Above the crowds can be seen Carys Tea Dealers, and behind the second canopy the Grey Mare public house, which closed in 1957. The market, which was also known as Wheatsheaf Market, moved to the present site on Ashburner Street in 1932, and the Octagon Theatre now occupies the site.

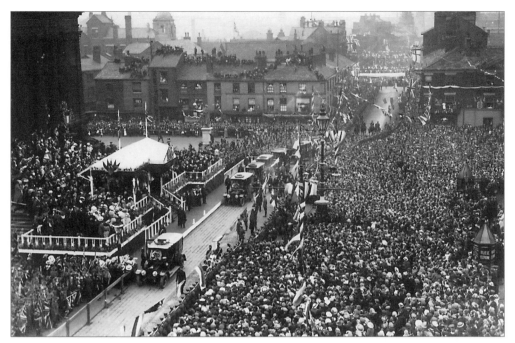

Vast crowds came to see King George V and Queen Mary in the Town Hall Square at 4.15 p.m. on 10 July 1913. The royal procession came down Higher Bridge Street, Saint Georges Road, Knowsley Street and Oxford Street before arriving at the Town Hall. The best views were from the rooftops around the square as this photograph, taken from the top of the Public Library (now the Nationwide Building Society), shows.

After being received at the Town Hall the royal party crossed to the Wholesale Market at about 4.40 p.m. to view an exhibition of Bolton-made goods and machinery. The textiles and machinery of Dobson and Barlow made up the largest part of the exhibition. There was also a programme of 'mass singing' by Bolton schoolchildren from the elementary schools.

Bolton from the air, probably *c.* 1927 as the slum clearance programme was nearing completion. The area in the centre was occupied by the first engineering works in Bolton, the Union Foundry of Rothwell and Hick, and also by the huge steelworks of Bessemers Ltd. The works were cleared by 1927 and Moor Lane bus station used the top part of the site from 1930. There is so much to see that it would need another book to describe everything. The time is late afternoon, and since you can just see the stalls at the wholesale fruit and vegetable market it is a Saturday.

own Hall and Civic Centre, after October 1934 when the Police Department to the north of the new Civic Centre
as completed. The Public Health Department was opened along with the Public Library in 1938. It would be
941 before the Museum opened, but the official opening by the Earl of Derby was in 1939. The extension to the
ld Town Hall of 1873 was almost complete, and to look at the whole today it is difficult to believe the Town Hall
as originally that small black building in the centre.

Victoria Square, 1928. This pair of semi-detached houses was sited very centrally and conveniently in the Civic Centre. They were Andrews 'Savework' houses, the very latest in housing design, erected during Civic Week on a site which is now the police station in Le Mans Crescent. Admission to view inside was 3d and the proceeds went to the Infirmary. The houses were taken down after Civic Week and never reappeared.

Loyal subjects of Her Majesty the Queen on her visit to Bolton in October 1954. They are watching the Queen inspecting the Royal North Lancashire Regiment in the centre of Victoria Square and are lucky enough to have a grandstand view from the Town Hall steps. The lady in the centre of the group on the right doesn't seem to mind the rain, but those in the large group photograph have dressed wisely for October. Note the '50s fashion accessory, the Pacamac.

idgway Fold, *c.* 1895. This small 'fold' of only eight cottages in the centre of town was only 200 ft from the main
oor of the Market Hall. The photographer had his back to the River Croal, and was looking south. There was also
Ridgway Court approached by Ridgway Gates off Deansgate: all the names derived from Thomas Ridgway,
pioneering Bolton bleacher who owned land here in the 1780s.

pposite, above: Back Cheapside, early 1880. Just off the Town Hall Square was, and still is, this narrow cobbled
treet leading south down to Great Moor Street. Most of the little shops and houses to the left have been
emolished but many of the stone backyards to the right remain to the rear of the modern frontages of Newport
treet (or Shoe Alley). The shop on the left is Walter Parkinson's umbrella shop and hairdressers, which was not
n uncommon combination at the time when gents' hairdressers sold walking sticks, canes, pipes and cigars. The
ain entrance to the shop was in Exchange Street round the corner.

elow: Bolton from the park on a remarkably smoke-free day, looking south-east to the town centre with the
ecreation ground to the right, 26 May 1904. The park of 56 acres was opened in 1862 by the Earl of Bradford
ho gave the land, and it cost £58,269. The name Queen's Park was given in 1897 on the occasion of Queen
ictoria's Jubilee.

Saint Helena Mill and the River Croal from the Central Street area, looking towards Tanners Bridge at the bottom of King Street, 1969. The area to the left is now the new BT telephone exchange. The earliest cotton mills in Bolton were in this area 200 years ago when the Croal was a small, clean stream. The mills used water to power their mules either directly from a water wheel or by pumping into ponds or reservoirs by steam power. The mill in the centre is on the site of Bolton's first mill, built in 1780 by bleacher James Thweat. It became known as Saint Helena Mill after 1815 and the Battle of Waterloo, perhaps because the mill was on a little island in the Croal. The oldest part still remains.

Exchange Street from Acresfield, looking towards the Town Hall, 1969. The street still exists and even a little bridge remains, although it is a new structure, but the whole area to the right is now the south part of the Arndale Centre, opened in 1971. Acresfield Mall in the centre keeps the name alive even though Acresfield and Back Acres have disappeared. The streets on the left are Back Mawdsley Street and Back Cheapside, which still exist. This photograph shows the Grapes Hotel bridge at the rear of the hotel which fronted on to Victoria Square. It was built in about 1846 and used to advertise 'Fine Old Ales and all the daily, illustrated and comic papers'. It was demolished in 1960, and the site was redeveloped to include Bolton's first Wimpy bar.

Harp Garage, previously the Harp Tavern, Moor Lane, 1973. The Harp, a Magee Marshall house from at least 1905, closed in 1913 and became a garage, Harp Garage, second right. This pub was a very popular local for the workers of Flash Street Mills just down the street, which closed in 1960 having been busiest about sixty years before. Users of the Sainsbury store now on the site may be interested to puzzle out where the pub was prior to demolition in 1973.

The Olympia roller-skating rink in Spa Road opened in September 1909 and closed in 1912. In May that year it reopened as the Olympia picture house. Two name changes followed: it became the Regal Cinema in September 1929, and the Astor Cinema on 12 November 1952. This postcard marks the opening of the Navada roller-skating rink in the same building in November 1952. Until destroyed by fire in September 1985, it was enjoyed by hundreds of skaters every week.

Trinity Street station, 1918. The station was originally opened by the Manchester, Bolton and Bury Canal Navigation in 1838 to service the growing rail links created by the pioneer George Stephenson. This was ten years after the opening of the Bolton to Leigh line, and two years before the Manchester to Liverpool line. The station was rebuilt in the late 1890s when the old bridge and road across the line were widened in order to accommodate a new booking hall, circulating area, parcels office and a cab approach, seen here. It was again rebuilt in 1903–4 with a tram terminal on the bridge but retaining the cab approach. The bridge was entirely replaced in 1968, and in 1987 a new station was opened 110 yards away in Newport Street, with no car parking facilities.

Very old property to the west side of Moor Lane, just prior to demolition when the area was being cleared for industrial development, c. 1900. To the right are St Paul's Church and Sunday School, built in 1865 to serve what was then an increasing congregation of about seven thousand people from Moor Lane, Spring Gardens and Howell Croft. Next to the Sunday School is the little lane leading to Taylor Fold. The warehouse on the left belonged to Harry Mason and Sons, who advertised as 'Builders' Merchants, Fireplaces and Tiling, Moor Lane (near Fire Station)'.

Harold Wilson, who was later to become Labour prime minister, walking between Great Moor Street and Newport Street towards the Town Hall, 1935. Mr Wilson had been to see Walter Street, bricklayer and contractor at 17 Great Moor Street. Just visible is the back of the O tram from Chorley Old Road to Trinity Street railway station.

Spa Road Recreation Ground, Queen's Park, 1918. The children of all the local schools were assembled here for a grand celebration to mark the end of the First World War. They were drilled here for weeks to assemble into various formations such as flags, the numbers 1918 and ending with a crown shape. In the background to the left is the Spa Road Electricity Works of 1914 and St Paul's Church.

This postcard of the Infirmary with an unusual blue background was sent to a Miss Findlow of Macclesfield, and was posted on 16 September 1908 at 7.15 p.m. Unusually the message space is blank and the words 'I am just taking baby out' are on the front. There is no signature.

This fascinating card of the Infirmary has a superimposed biplane skimming the rooftops. The Infirmary, off Chorley New Road, was opened in 1883 with the closure of the Nelson Square building, and became Bolton Royal Infirmary in 1931. Various extensions were added up to 1964 with names commemorating Sir Winston Churchill, Barnes, Cooper, Mallett, Patrick (local worthies), Chadwick (doctor) and Kitchener. The fine old building closed in late 1996, and Bolton General Hospital is now on a new site. Other cards of this type are known, and date from about 1916 to 1917 when the Infirmary was closed to the public (except for emergencies) and four extra wards in tents were set up on the lawn for wounded soldiers. The postcard might be the work of a talented inmate of that time.

Davenport Street off Vernon Street. This sequence of photographs shows slum housing before the clearances tha
took place between 1916 and 1927. Various types of houses are shown, most of the 'back-to-back' type whic
crammed most houses into the smallest space and were speculatively built by builders at the lowest possible cost i
the late Victorian era. Those that existed before 1860 were the target of a campaign by Doctors Ferguson an
Chadwick, in particular the cellar dwellings where a twelfth of the population of central Bolton lived. This ha
come about after handloom weaving disappeared and the cellars fell vacant; they became separate dwellings for a
average of four people.

Slum clearance has ensured that these dwellings are now only a memory.

Howarth's Court off Nut Street, off Halliwell Road, 1918. Of all the residents living here in 1918 only one family was not employed in the cotton trade.

Mercer's Court, 1916.

Opposite: Green's Court, 1927. Situated off Chorley Street, this is now the site of Bolton Royal Infirmary car park. Some of the oldest and worst slum dwellings were to be found in this area. The single gas lamp was the only source of illumination for the whole of Green's Court.

Back Green's Court, 1918. This was an unusually spacious count for a back street, with the added advantage of a gas lamp. The curving profile shows that the buildings followed an ancient boundary rather than the buildings speculatively built by mill owners after 1850. The court seems to have been solely housing with no evidence of handloom weaving.

Edge's Court, off Central Street, Deansgate, 1919. The two cottages to the left were typical handloom weavers' cottages with the loom being worked in the cellar and the front door two or three steps up to give height to the cellar. The area is now a car park.

CHAPTER TWO

BELMONT, EDGWORTH & CHAPELTOWN

The stone masons who worked on the Congregational Church in Belmont which opened in 1899. The head mason (in the bowler hat on the left) and his family lodged in the village at Maria Square for four years until work was completed. Maria Square was the first row of cottages to be built, in what is still a pretty moorland village, in 1804 by Thomas Ryecroft who owned the local textile printing works. Maria was the name of his daughter.

Stonemasons outside the Blackburn Road United Reform Church, 1897. It was originally named Blackburn Road Congregational Church and began in 1872 as a branch of the St George's Road church in two cottages in Blackbank Street. Most Boltonians know the church as the 'Iron Church' but do not know why. In 1878 a sectional corrugated-iron building was purchased and planted on this site, and was used until this building was opened in 1897. It was largely financed by W.H. Lever, the first Lord Leverhulme.

The National Children's Homes at Edgworth, just 7 miles north of Bolton town centre on the moors, also known as Crowthorn School or The Children's Home on the Moors. The land for the Homes was donated by James Barlow JP, and the building was inaugurated in August 1873. The nucleus of the Homes was the Wheatsheaf Inn and a stone on the front of the original building still bears the name, although it was rebuilt in 1923. The Homes had a model dairy, metal workshop, model bakery, swimming baths, joiners' shop, sewing room and even a clogger's shop. The Homes are still there. These popular cards produced by the Children's Home and Orphanage, Lancashire Branch, date from 1905 and were on sale in Bolton to bolster funds.

The orphans' Whit Sunday procession.

A general, probably posed, view of the school looking north up to Broadhead.

The craft class at Crowthorn. Woodwork and bookbinding were among the subjects taught. Every boy had a clean white shirt and waistcoat.

The bakery. As well as learning a trade the orphans produced bread for the whole school plus a surplus to sell in the area.

Members of St Anne's church in Chapeltown, a few miles north of Bolton, assembling outside the Chethams Arms before their Field Day, 1914. The male choir is preparing to sing to the music of the Eagley Mills band. Field Days, run by the church Sunday School, were held regularly in the summer months almost always without tents or marquees, and the day would include races for prizes such as books and pencil sets. They were sometimes held in May to coincide with the May Queen and Maypole celebrations: the male equivalent of the May Queen was traditionally named the Earl Marshal.

CHAPTER THREE

ASTLEY BRIDGE &
TONGE MOOR

Hall i' th' Wood, 1909. The name is pronounced Allitwood locally. The wood has long since vanished. The hall was built by a wealthy clothier, Lawrence Brownlow, in the 1480s; he had a fulling mill at nearby Eagley Brook where he finished his cloth. A stone wing to the left was added in 1591 but the stone front dates from 1648. When Samuel Crompton was five in 1758 his family came to live here, and tradition has it that he invented his Mule in the little room just above the doorway on the left. The hall was occupied by various families at this time and had become run down. It continued to be so until W.H. Lever, the Boltonian and first Lord Leverhulme, bought it and presented it to the town as a museum in 1899.

Firwood Fold – the birthplace on 3 December 1753 of Samuel Crompton (1753–1827), inventor of the world-famous cotton spinning machine, the Mule. Firwood was a small farm owned for several generations by Cromptons just 2 miles from Bolton town centre, but at this time many farmers in Lancashire were starting to combine farming with manufacturing – some without success, like Samuel's father. The property was mortgaged to the Starkies of Huntroyde.

Blackburn Road, Astley Bridge, 1906. Prominent opposite Tram D to Dunscar is the Tippings Arms. Further down is the Cornbrook Ales railway hotel, so named because of the junction at Astley Bridge station down Waters Meeting Road. Just over the bridge down to the right was Heywood's Hollow and one of the earliest local bleachworks, Waters Meeting Bleach Works, which ran from 1853 to 1962.

Opposite, above: A separate Housing Department was set up in 1930, and by 1938, at a total capital cost of £2¼ million, 5,555 council houses had been built. The first estate was Platt Hill, Green Lane, then the Firwood Estate shown here, whose houses cost an average all-in price of £1,000. Gross rent was 16s 10d.

Below: Little Bolton Hall, just off Folds Road, down Turner Street, *c.* 1960. The original hall dated back to around 1300, but this was the latest building – rebuilt by Stephen Blair of Mill Hill Bleachworks in 1862. It was presented along with five cottages to St John's Church by F. Beatrice Blair on 16 May 1907 and was well used, but slowly became run down and was demolished during the summer of 1960. The wall with the Blair initials and crest could still be seen thirteen years ago. The Hall is often confused with Little Bolton Town Hall, All Saints Street.

Kay Street and Turton Street, 1880s. The photograph is taken from the north corner of Union Street, looking towards the Falcon Inn on the right and the Black Horse beer house on the left at the corner of Falcon Street. The day is almost certainly a Sunday and the occasion is a sermon by a revivalist preacher, probably one of the many American preachers who held open-air meetings all over Victorian England. The area was entirely working-class, dominated by Kay Street Machine Works and Globe Foundry, but there seems little evidence of working men in attendance. Some women in the foreground wear the Lancashire shawl.

CHAPTER FOUR

GREAT LEVER, DARCY LEVER & LITTLE LEVER

Looking east to Green Lane and Bradford Road, 1925–30. The building in the very centre is the Fishpool Institution, opened as a workhouse in 1861. To the left is Townleys Hospital, opened on 1 March 1899 on land bought from the Townleys Estate. Townleys Hall is just across the railway from Great Moor Street station to Little Hulton. Bottom right can be seen the Hollins Cottage Homes, which separated from the workhouse in 1914. It had cottages and a nursery for 120 children. The whole area below the railway line is now Royal Bolton Hospital, opened in the mid-1990s.

olton Board of Guardians, 1927. The Board of Guardians for what was the old County Borough was set up on February 1837 as a result of the Poor Law Amendment Act of 1834. Seen here are the Guardians responsible or Hollins Cottage Homes. In the doorway arch to the left is Father Cornwell, and below and to his right is Mrs Marshall, Justice of the Peace. A group of well-scrubbed boys have been assembled for the photograph.

Darcy Lever Old Hall, early twentieth century. It was Robert Lever of Darcy Lever, a wealthy London clothier with local connections who provided funds to build Bolton Grammar School in his will of 1641. The Civil War delayed the legal work but by 1658 the school was built in the church grounds; it stood here until 1880. The hall remained as a farmhouse (as seen here) for many years until demolition in 1950, although the outline may still be traced.

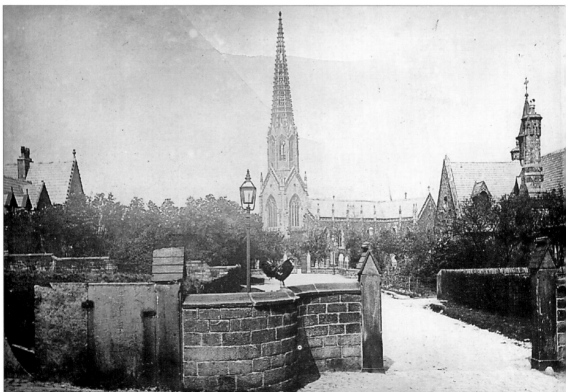

Saint Stephen and All Martyrs' Church, school and vicarage, Lever Bridge, near Darcy Lever. These buildings were constructed almost entirely from the material excavated from John Fletcher's Ladyshore Colliery, just down the nearby canal, and fired on site to become terracotta bricks and intricate mouldings. Between 1842 and 1845 the architect John Sharpe converted all the fired clay into a beautiful church with a delicate open-work spire based on that of Fribourg Cathedral, and even used terracotta for the organ case and font. It was found later that the material became porous and twisted over time, resulting in most of the spire, the vicarage and school being demolished. The church, which cost £3,000 to build, has recently been fully restored.

Hag End Brow, Darcy Lever, 1927. The bridge spanning the rivers Croal and Tonge, and Bradshaw Brook just upstream to the left, was being altered. In the centre is the railway bridge of the Liverpool, Bolton & Bury line of 1848, which was reconstructed in 1881 with a span of 72 ft. Below it is Lever Bridge Mills and Dam Side Mill, built in 1784. This was as far as Bolton Corporation trams came, and the end of the line is just visible. The service ended in 1928.

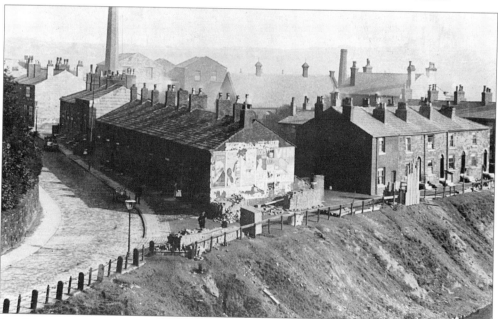

Radcliffe Road from the Damside Aqueduct, Darcy Lever, early 1900s. The aqueduct was a remarkable construction of which very few illustrations are available. It carried the Bolton, Bury & Manchester canal 91 yards over the Croal valley and was opened in 1791. Hacken Mills, built in about 1850 by James Wardle, are in the background. By 1884 there were 520 power looms. The village is a good example of a water-powered industrial community later converted to steam power, and was fed by three coal mines within a quarter of a mile.

Whit Walks, Little Lever, 1911. The procession, led by Bolton Borough Prize Band, is just passing George Street. Working-class families would scrimp and save for these occasions, when the little Sunday School girls were called 'little singers' and they had to have a white dress, new shoes and socks no matter what the state of the family economy was.

CHAPTER FIVE

MOSES GATE & FARNWORTH

Moses Gate, Farnworth, Whit Friday 1896. This fine sunny day was the walking day of St Gregory's School, Farnworth. The ladies are dressed in their Sunday best. The marching band was Barnes's Mill Band from Farnworth, and the whole procession had just passed Moses Gate station on Bolton Road.

Moses Gate, between 1936 and 1938. Two F trams are crossing, one going to Black Horse, Farnworth, the other to Bolton. Horse-drawn trams ran here from the late 1870s, the last one on 1 January 1900, and from then on electric trams ran to Moses Gate (but not to Farnworth) until 1902. These trams are the old Urban District Council ones, later sold to South Lancashire Tramways and only replaced by buses in 1944. The LMS Moses Gate railway station building and stationmaster's house have been replaced by just a bus shelter and platform. The two public houses still remain, with Magee Marshall's Railway on the left and Seed and Co.'s Moses Gate Hotel on the right. Accurate dating is possible because the public toilets on the left were erected in 1936, and Seed's brewery was taken over by Dutton Ltd in 1938.

The funeral of Robert Smith of Rawson Street, Farnworth, August 1907. The fact that the well-turned-out hearse was horse-drawn was appropriate since Mr Smith was a conductor on the horse-drawn omnibus service from Bolton to Manchester in the late 1890s.

Birch House, Farnworth, was built in 1641 and stood at the centre of Bolton Road and Gladstone Road: a garage is now opposite the site. Old Farnworthians used to call it Gladstone Villas after the Rt Hon. W.E. Gladstone. After occupation by many distinguished local families the house began to decline, and was offered for rent in 1897 – when the contents, including armour, the library paintings and carved oak, were auctioned. Another auction of contents followed in 1950 prior to demolition in the mid-1950s, although tradition has it that the Adam-style doorway (behind the porch in the painting) was saved by the Council.

The circus comes to town, Farnworth, 23 April 1898. Lord John Sanger's circus gave two performances on the Market Ground. The procession is just at the spot where Farnworth Library stands today; Birch House is in the background. As well as the chariots and horses there were elephants, lions, camels and 'curiosities'.

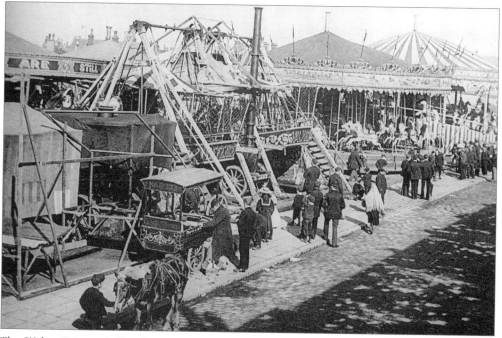

The Wakes Fair, probably also 1898. All the rides are steam-powered and above the ice-cream seller's barrow are the swing boats or 'steam yachts' as they were then called; they were considered dangerous at the time to both occupants and bystanders. To the right of those are two sets of 'steam gallopers', which can still be seen at specialist steam fairs today.

Greetings from Farnworth: this card was posted at 6 p.m. on 12 July 1924 to Mrs Haslam at the Home of Rest, Fairhaven, Lytham St Annes, from Elsie, Tom and Father with the aim of cheering Mrs Haslam up. Elsie writes: 'The doctor has changed my medicine but it's done me no good. I feel a bit better this morning but I'm not fit. Tom says the bowling green's rotten.' These are meant to be the five best views of Farnworth, with the secondhand rag market in the centre, two views of the park, the Town Hall and the Carnegie Library.

At the same time as the adoption of the Local Government Act Farnworth gained its first public park, opened by W.E. Gladstone, then Chancellor of the Exchequer, in 1864. Most of the money and all of the land came from Mr Thomas Barnes, local cotton merchant and owner of the Birch Hall estate. Even with the low land values of the day it was worth £11,000 for the 12 acres, and Mr Barnes spent another £2,000 laying out the park. Since it was autumn when it opened all the local people picked the remaining flowers in their gardens to add to the colour.

The card shows four little girls sitting below the Barnes Memorial. Barnes's mill chimneys are behind.

The secondhand clothes market between King Street and Brackley Street behind the Bowling Green Hotel, Farnworth, early 1900s. Both photographs illustrate the typical dress of women at the time, with long skirt, white apron and of course the essential Lancashire shawl worn as a head covering. Both photographs are by J. Pickford: the one above was made into a postcard.

John Collier's Shop, 79 Glynne Street, Farnworth, *c.* 1910. Mary Alice Collier and her son John Boardman Collier are outside their butcher's shop. The shop is typical of a small local butcher's shop, and was located in a working-class area of miners and mainly textile workers, many of whom would be employed in Barnes Dixon Green Mill opposite the shop.

A flock of sheep is being driven from Salford to be slaughtered at the rear of John Collier's shop in Glynne Street, *c.* 1910. This was a common occurrence which continued until the 1950s, with both sheep and cattle being herded through the streets.

CHAPTER SIX

RINGLEY, KEARSLEY & DARLEY

This is a collection of prints from the lantern slides of John W. Pickford, a Farnworth journalist from 1884 to 1927, who lived in Rawson Street. The slides were taken on a cartridge Kodak 1898 model and date from 1907. They show Ringley Mayor-making: this was a mock mayor-making ceremony enacted every year on the first Monday in May, and was little more than a pub crawl in fancy dress around the seven pubs of Ringley. They are unusual for their time since they show movement and action, not the usual posed groups. The mayor outside the Three Crowns, the first port of call. Thomas Warburton was the landlord. *Above*: The mayor and his four supporters drank here for free. The mayor's costume is an old military tunic and the mace a toasting fork and crust.

The mayor and retinue entering the Three Crowns under the stalls and games tables. The right-hand stall was selling 'milkey [*sic*] coconuts as low as 3*d*'. The landlord from 1907 to 1911 was Joseph Davies, who advertised 'Good ales, bowling green and coffin maker'.

The mayor on his form crossing the seventeenth-century pack horse bridge over the River Irwell to the other side of the village. He holds the 'proclamation', which was really the Wakes programme of sports and games.

Safely over the bridge with the Three Crowns behind, and approaching the Lord Nelson on the second run. This is a good study of the onlookers in their Sunday best with clogs polished up. Even though it was a celebration day it was still Monday and washday, with a full line on the river bank.

Ringley Old Tower. It was rebuilt in 1827, incorporating the original church dedication stone, which read: 'Nathan Walworth Builded Mee Anno Do 1625'. The little shed to the left was a clogger's shop.

Just out of Ringley and into Kearsley on what is now the A666, looking west to Farnworth, 1907. The tramway system to Clifton was operated by Farnworth UDC until 1906 when the South Lancashire Tramways Company took it over. Here worn rails are being replaced.

When the tramway men had gone home the children of the Halshaw Lane area came out to play on what the workmen had left. This is now the roundabout on the A666 over St Peter's Way in Farnworth.

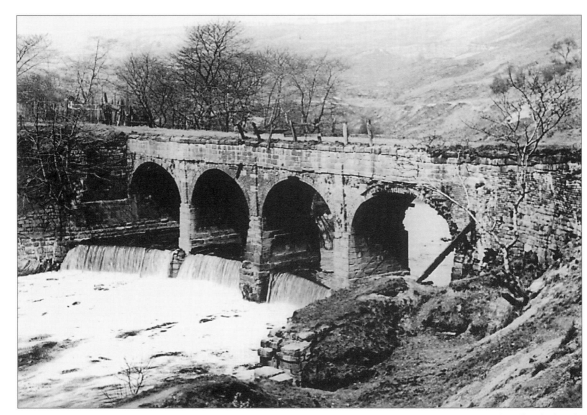

Oakes Bridge over the River Croal, 1907. The bridge was built in about 1790 of stone with a brick finish, presumably by Benjamin Rawson as a means of access to his chemical works near Nob End. The associated weir supplied water to the works. Two arches collapsed in the 1940s, and the bridge was finally demolished entirely in 1990.

CHAPTER SEVEN

OVER HULTON

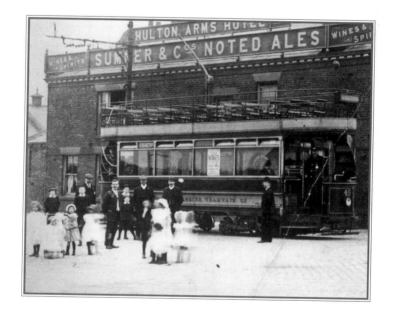

Plodder Lane, with the junction of Watergate Lane to the left, *c*. 1930. This area is known as Edge Fold; before 1850 this part of Plodder Lane was known as Scalyard Lane. The hamlet was an outlying coalmining district, which exploited the valuable Cannel seam from about 1720 onwards on land belonging to the Hulton family. Sandstone was also quarried here until the present century by Jackson's Stone Quarries. The Bridgewater underground canal system reached Edge Fold (with the Upper Navigable Level) in the early nineteenth century, and five mines were worked in the area although not all connected to the canal. It was possible in the early years of the nineteenth century to take a barge of coal from under the centre of the area shown here to Worsley near Manchester in five hours – all underground.

Plodder Lane, just past Edge Fold at the junction of Smethurst Lane, in the bad winter of 1947. The snow was up to the tops of the gas lamps.

St Helens Road, looking south towards Four Lane Ends (sometimes called Hulton Lane Ends), *c.* 1910. In the distance is the R tram back to Bolton, which was operated by Bolton Corporation Tramways from 1902 to 1936 on this route. The continuation to Atherton and Leigh was run by South Lancashire Tramways. To the extreme left is Plodder Lane to Farnworth. The M61 motorway now runs in a cutting from left to right across the centre of the picture. To the left of the tram is the Red Lion Hotel and to the right the Hulton Arms, with its popular bowling green.

The Hulton Arms Hotel at Four Lane Ends, 1906. The hotel was extensively altered after this date to cater for the increasing coach and charabanc trade passing along the main A6 road to Preston and Blackpool. The brewery of John Sumner & Co. Ltd was at the Haigh Brewery near Wigan. It was founded before 1851 and was taken over by Greenall Whitley & Co. Ltd of Warrington in 1931. The open-topped tram going to Bolton has a poster for Tyldesley Wakes in the window.

CHAPTER EIGHT

DEANE

Deane Road, looking west from the tower of St Saviour's Church, Deane, at the point where Deane Road becomes Wigan Road, *c.* 1910. To the right is the site of the Diamond Brewery of William Tong and Sons, and next uphill is Green Bank Farm, then three private houses: The Holly, The Elms and Whitebank (home of Joshua Crook, manufacturer in 1841). The factory to the left is that of Henry Poole and Co. Ltd, cotton spinners at Deane Mill. Today both sides of this road are heavily built up.

Deane Church, Deane, on Sermons Day, *c.* 1890. The crowd is gathered around the ancient yew tree which is no longer there. This church and the parish church were the only ones in existence locally until the chapel of ease at Bradshaw was built in 1560. Deane and Dean Moor were once very wild places. Dr James Black wrote in 1837: 'Dean Moor is now crossed by the traveller without fear of being slutched or stoned by the wild natives, or of having to encounter those haggard infernal sprites the Buggarts.'

Tom Sanderson, Deane Church, early 1900s. Mr Sanderson was verger and gravedigger at Deane Church for many years. He was born on 29 February 1868, and it was his proud boast that as it was a leap year he had celebrated only nineteen birthdays before 1948, when he was eighty. The graveyard is not as tidy now as in Tom's day and the ancient yew behind him has gone.

Punch Street and Ardwick Street, 1941. On 12 October 1941 two 500 kilo high explosive bombs fell in this area at the bottom of Deane Road, killing eleven people and injuring sixty-four. The factory of Bolton Heald Co. Ltd was totally destroyed, as was part of Joshua Crook Ltd on Dean Road. Eighty houses were rendered uninhabitable and 300 premises, mostly homes, were damaged, some of them half a mile away. The first attack on Bolton in the Second World War was on 9 January 1941, when a single bomb fell at the corner of Crook Street and Burns Street, destroying four houses and Jimmy's Cafe. The last attack was in April 1942 when eighteen bombs and incendiaries fell on the lower part of Smithills Dean. The lorry shown above belonged to the Council Streets Department.

Opposite: On the night of 25–26 September 1916 Bolton was attacked from the air by a Zeppelin, which came in from the north and bombed Holcombe. Most damage was done in Kirk Street, lower Deane Road area, where thirteen people were killed and dozens injured and made homeless. The same Zeppelin bombed Apple Street, Lodge Vale (Mortfield), Hobart Street, Waldeck Street, Wellington Yard, Back John Street, Queen's Park, Holy Trinity Church, Hardcastle's Mill in Parrot Street, Acresfield and Old Hall Street, all with little damage.

The emergency food van was provided by the Ford Motor Company and maintained at no cost by Gordons of Bolton. It is seen here on 12 October 1941.

CHAPTER NINE

SMITHILLS, BARROW BRIDGE & HALLIWELL

The Colliers Arms, Chorley Old Road, 1931. The photographer looks back up the hill towards Horwich on the road which became 'turnpiked' in 1763 after passing through the toll bar cottage at Doffcocker (which still exists). The area was a small self-contained mining village with the principal pits at Delph Hill, which in common with many other local collieries produced fireclay. The chimney to the left of the picture belonged to Doffcocker Fireclay Co., sanitary pipe and firebrick manufacturers. The Colliers Arms' landlord at this time was William Gleave.

Bob's Smithy, Chorley Old Road, 1931. This is now a popular public house, but is seen here as a two-room beer house just prior to the road-widening scheme which did away with the forge and smithy to the right of the picture. The landlord in 1931 was Emile Carnes. The road had been improved under the Turnpike Acts in 1763, and a new road to Horwich had been constructed in 1824.

Barrow Bridge and Sixty-three Steps. A popular day-trip destination in the twentieth century, the area was one of Bolton's earliest and, later, largest cotton enterprises known then as Dean Mills. The old estate of Dean Mills was purchased by Robert Gardner in 1831. He was later joined by Thomas Bazley and became Gardner & Bazley in 1843. By 1846 the 1,000 workers had good houses, some with gardens, a canteen, baker, library, co-operative shop and educational institute. It was a 'model village' and in 1851 was visited by Prince Albert. Various problems forced the Dean Mills Co. into bankruptcy in 1895 and by 1913 almost no trace was left.

Barrow Bridge Mills, during demolition in 1913.

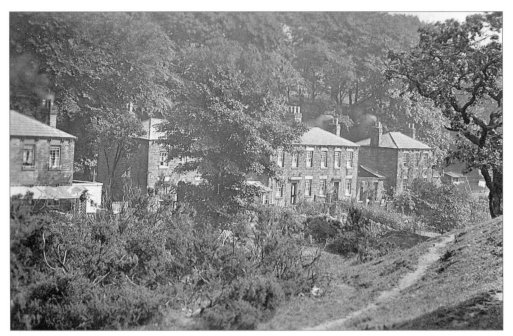

Barrow Bridge became the 'Deserted Village', visited by thousands of Edwardian day-trippers and later generations when the nearby Moss Bank Park opened in 1922. It is now a quiet residential area less than 3 miles from Bolton town centre.

Sixty-three Steps, Barrow Bridge. An early Edwardian picnic.

Doffcockers, 1909. This house, named after the mid-eighteenth-century hamlet a few miles west of Bolton, was originally the home of a Mr Whitaker, proprietor of Doffcocker Mill. It was later owned by Sir Benjamin Dobson, who made considerable alterations. After his death the hall passed through several ownerships and in 1909 great plans were announced to turn the house and grounds into a 'White City', with the house becoming a tearooms and billiard saloon. In the face of great opposition the plans were scrapped and Doffcockers was demolished in 1913. The house name lives on in the area, and its site is still known locally as Doffies Wood.

Church Road, Halliwell, looking east towards Bennetts Lane (to the left), late 1890s. The houses to the left, which today still display traces of the curved woodwork, were probably built in the early 1890s when Church Road was being developed. Just before this group of houses is Alma Bank, which has a terracotta datestone of 1889. The large building in the centre is No. 26 branch of the Great and Little Bolton Co-operative Society (established 1859); it is little altered externally today. The resolution for the branch was passed on Monday 27 August 1894: That the seal of the Society be affixed between Oliver Ormrod of the first part, Knowles Edge of the second part, and this Society. . .'.

Lodge Vale, Mortfield Lane, after the raid of 25 September 1916. Three people were in the house and miraculously none was injured. The Zeppelin was the L21, built in 1915, and one of seven to cross the east coast that night, although it is thought their navigation was faulty. L21, Commander Frankenburg and its crew were shot down in November 1916 near Yarmouth.

CHAPTER TEN

HORWICH & RIVINGTON

A deserted early morning Lee Lane, Horwich, before 1908. In that year the Victoria Road, Lee Lane tram N still ran to the Crown Hotel at the junction of Chorley Old and New Roads.

A group of workers in the yard of Wallsuches Bleachworks, on Chorley Old Road, Horwich, c. 1888. A very early bleachworks, utilising the moorland streams and local coal seams, it was built in 1777 by John and Thomas Ridgway, only passing into the control of the Bleachers' Association Ltd in 1925. It still remains an important industrial archaeological site and has been very little altered, still with the central clocktower and various reservoirs. It is currently used in part by Arcon Engineering.

Bridge Foot Smithy, Horwich, *c.* 1888. This is the rural side of Horwich in contrast to the southern side where in the mid-1880s the Lancashire and Yorkshire Railway workshop was established. In ten years the population of Horwich went from 3,000 to 13,000. The smithy and the railway works closed in the 1980s, at almost the same time.

A well-turned-out travelling shop in the Horwich area, *c.* 1890. Travellers and itinerant shops were beginning to be replaced by the corner shop – itself a victim of circumstance 100 years later.

Joseph Robinson, a worker at Wallsuches Bleachworks
who lived at one of the Wallsuches Houses, 1880s.
Behind him are Park Reservoir and Chorley Old Road;
the area in which he is standing was known as Top o'
th' Wallsuches.

Brownlow Castle, Horwich, 1900s. Better known as Rockhaven and not a castle at all, the building
of 1840 dominated the Horwich skyline until demolition in May 1942. The nickname Brownlow
Castle was coined when a Bolton solicitor Richard Brownlow took the place and added battlements
to the building. The exposed position meant that few people stayed long and two of the occupiers,
Mr Brownlow who died in 1899 and a Dr Gilchrist from Bolton, were said to have contracted a
terrible disease, often described as leprosy.

Rivington is 7 miles west of Bolton and perhaps the most popular destination around for days out walking, climbing, fishing, sailing, para-gliding or just doing nothing. Much of the landscape owes the way it looks to the attentions of perhaps the most famous and remarkable Boltonian W.H. Lever, later Viscount Leverhulme. He was born in Wood Street off Bradshawgate in 1851 and at his death in 1925 his soap empire was worth £56 million. Leverhulme built the famous Bungalow on the shoulder of Bolton's most prominent landmark Rivington Pike and set about turning the wild moorland into what are still locally known as the Japanese (or Chinese) Gardens. There were terraced gardens, waterfalls, bridges, lakes, pagodas and a massive Pigeon Tower which still stands. He also purchased the massive Lever Park, Horwich, and the Rivington Hall estate with its two medieval barns, all of which Leverhulme presented to the people of Bolton as a park. This is a view of the Bungalow after it was burned down in 1913 following an arson attack by a suffragette from Preston. This was doubly unfortunate since Leverhulme supported the cause. The site was used for a second bungalow built in stone which, after Leverhulme's death, was bought by Thomas Magee, one of the Bolton brewers. It was demolished in 1948 but traces of some of the tiled floors can still be seen.

Looking south from the ornamental gardens over Lower Rivington reservoir and across to Blackrod. In the centre right on the shores of the reservoir the replica of Liverpool Castle can just be seen. Leverhulme had this built deliberately as a ruin, partly to alleviate local unemployment and partly as a focal point to be viewed from the Bungalow. The castle still remains much as it was when finished.

CHAPTER ELEVEN

COAL MINING

Pretoria Pit, otherwise known as No. 3 Bank Pit of Hulton Collieries. On 21 December 1910 344 men and boys lost their lives – more in a single day than the Oaks Pit disaster in Yorkshire in December 1866. The cause was thought to be gas from a roof fall ignited by an overheated lamp, with coal dust explosion a further factor. Westhoughton lost 203 colliers, Daubhill 61, Bolton 8 and the rest came from Atherton, Tyldesley, Chequerbent, the Hultons, Walkden, Westleigh and Hindley Green.

Collecting for the Mayor's Pretoria Fund. G.W. Lloyd, taxidermist of 145 Derby Street, Bolton, on the Town Hall steps collected money with the help of his large collection of mounted specimens of lions, tigers, zebras and other animals. The fund reached £88,400, and Mr Lloyd received a commendation from the King and Queen.

A tableau constructed to help raise money for the Pretoria Fund, probably one of Mr Lloyd's creations mounted on Hulton Colliery's rolling stock. A model coalface is shown, with a collier undercutting a coalface and a boy in front of a loaded tub. This would be quite a good high seam to work in at Pretoria: most were much lower.

Pretoria Pit Commemorative Serviette, 1911. There were only three survivors of the disaster: J. Sharples and two youngsters, J. Staveley and W. Davenport. Most of the dead are buried in a mass grave in Westhoughton churchyard: twenty-four bodies were unidentified at the time of burial.

Great Lever Colliery, from Raikes Lane looking north, *c.* 1920. The colliery was owned by the Earl of Bradford and was sunk in 1828, reaching the Cannel seam at 1,680 ft. Never a successful venture because of expensive pumping operations and lack of demand for high class coal, closure was inevitable in April 1922. Some of the pithead buildings can still be seen at the old greyhound track site opened in 1927.

Victoria Colliery was founded in 1866 by John and Thomas Rosbottom on land leased from Sir Charles Tempest (grandfather of Baroness Beaumont). Victoria was the smallest colliery in the area and was never mechanised, all coal being won by hand. The shaft was 75 yards deep and workings extended 230 yards at an average gradient of 1 in 7. The only seam worked was the 3 ft 6 in Arley, which was almost fault free. Victoria closed on 14 October 1960.

CHAPTER TWELVE

TRANSPORT

A horse-drawn outing from the Leigh Arms in Blackrod to the popular beauty spot and refreshment rooms at the top of Parbold Hill, early 1900s. Most popular local wagonettes were operated by Holden's of Bolton.

Two horse-drawn omnibuses and a private carriage, 1905. The group posed here were all part of a private party organised by John H. Bromilow of Bark Street Garage en route to the annual point-to-point races near Chorley. The races are no longer run.

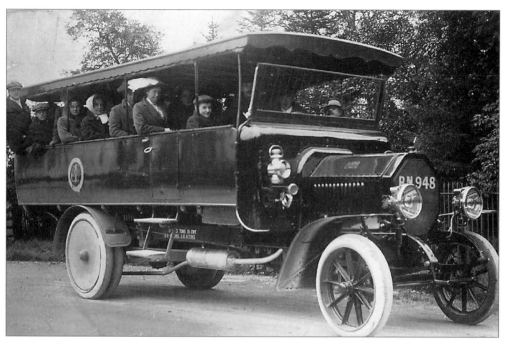

The 'Lady Evelyn' charabanc, taking an excursion from Heaton Tennis Club, August 1911. Another of Bromilow's fleet, the 'Lady Evelyn' could also be converted to a flatbed lorry.

A Milnes-Daimler (Mercedes) charabanc seen here in flatbed lorry form, 1910. It was also registered to John H. Bromilow, by this date General Carrier of Churchgate. The Churchgate premises later became Fletcher's Church House Garage, partly on the site of the old vicarage of St Peter's.

BN 101 is thought to be a 1904 Clement Talbot, registered in Bolton and belonging to a local colliery manager. It is pictured in about 1910 in Trafford Park near Barton Power Station with all the family on board.

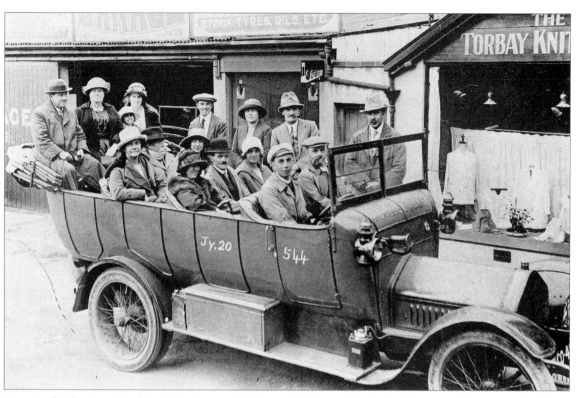

A party of Boltonians in a hired charabanc at Torbay, probably on a local church-organised outing, early 1920s. The weather protection was very limited. The hood would be fairly easy to erect but the side screens with their mica panels would only be deployed by the driver in the most serious of deluges. The driver was usually attired in a substantial leather motoring coat, hat and gauntlets.

Opposite: BN 838 on a fine sunny day in the country. In the registration books of the old Borough the vehicle is described as a 20 hp Beeston Humber, first owned by Richardson Tuer and Co. Ltd of Egerton Street, Farnworth, who ran Hope Foundry. There were two different bodies, one a five-seat open tourer and the other a six-seat three-quarter landaulette, both in dark blue with pale blue lining and black moulding. The car was first registered on 28 February 1912 and the photograph dates from soon after this date.

Regulars and family from the Park Inn, Farnworth, on a charabanc trip, 1920s. This group are at their first port of call, the popular Squirrel public house on the A673, probably en route for Blackpool. There appear to be over thirty people on board.

Charabanc of J. Battersby & Sons, summer 1924. No details are known but the destination was probably Blackpool. Edith, a local lady, recalls: 'We used to save up sixpence a week 'till we'd got five shillings. All t' family and some of t' neighbours would too and we used to take a charra, take our sandwiches for a day trip to Blackpool. All the charras would line up on Victoria Square ready . . . and you just got on the one which took your fancy. What a to-do if it were rainin'.'

The fleet of lorries owned by John A. Walker, a cotton waste dealer at Nelson Square and Thynne Street from 1906 to 1908 and later at 48 Saville Street to just before 1920. The photograph above is of the yard at Thynne Street with the old Trinity Street railway station just visible in the distance. The picture below shows one of Walker's lorries, a solid tyred Alldays registered in Manchester as NA 5296. It is well roped and sheeted with a tarpaulin from John Wood's Bolton Tarpaulin Works in Breightmet Street. This shot is from the Saville Street yard, as just visible is St Peter's Church tower.

Trev. Barker's Trinity Motor Works at 158–60 Crook Street with a group of lady delivery drivers collecting lorries, during the Second World War. The vehicle nearest the camera is signwritten 'James Unsworth, Haulage Contractor, 350 Manchester Road, Westhoughton'. The trade plates are 081 BN and 059 BN. The Painters Arms at the end of the street still remains but not as a traditional pub. Originally a Magee's house it was bought by Hamer's Brewery, and subsequently became a Dutton's house before becoming Scandals in 1984. It is now closed.

Edge's works outing or picnic probably during Bolton holidays or wakes week, 1950. If the bundles on the roof of the left-hand coach are food for the picnic it would have been a good one. William Edge & Sons Ltd, Bolton, were world-famous, mainly for their Edge's Dolly Blue, a simple product but most effective on washday whites. Edge's also produced Dolly Cream, Drummer Dyes, Jiffy Dyes, Drummer Pine Disinfectant and Drummer Air Freshener.

CHAPTER THIRTEEN

HUMAN INTEREST & FASHION

Two proud sports teams, early 1900s. Very few of these photographs, turned into postcards presumably for team members, family and friends, have survived. The upper photograph shows the cricket team of Know Mill, Entwistle, who were textile printers of long standing. It appears that collar and tie were the order of the day, but some of the ties seem a little short. The lower photograph is of Eagley Institute football club, the winners of Bolton Charity Cup for the season 1903/4. It was taken by Cowley Brothers, who may be the same firm that developed an early aeroplane engine at Bella Street, Daubhill, in conjunction with A.V. Roe.

Boys playing marbles, early 1900s. Various locations have been suggested, and this is probably Great Lever. The games one could invent with a bag of marbles were many and varied, and could be played anywhere, especially in the back-to-back streets if players kept away from the drains.

J.K. Waite and family, early 1900s. James Kirkbride Waite (born 1829) was Librarian of Bolton from July 1870 to 1904. In the background is Chesham House where Waite lived. It was a fine three-storey stone building attached to Little Bolton Town Hall, Bolton's short-lived local history museum. Chesham House was demolished to make way for offices in the 1980s.

Sale day at a Rivington farm, *c.* 1890. Although the actual farm is not identifiable the picture is a good example of a farm sale when a farmer, fallen on hard times, sells up almost everything he possesses. This looks like the end of the sale when livestock and machinery has been sold and people are buying fleeces, a horsewhip and pottery (see bottom right). All the farmer's neighbours would come to buy, most paying over the odds and often for something they might not want, just to help out.

Blackrod National and Sunday School class, 1890s. Pupils and teachers are dressed in their best for the occasion. These National or British Schools grew from the successful Sunday School movement where many churches started day schools, some of which still exist. The Blackrod School opened in 1845, and in 1907 it became the Blackrod Parish Church of England School.

A group of young men outside Barnes and Aspinall's confectioners, Chorley Old Road, dressed in their Sunday best ready for an outing: straw boaters and canes were the order of the day. Confectioners' shops were on almost every street corner between 1900 and the Second World War, and at the time of the photograph there were almost 700 in the town, often combined with temperance bars selling non-alcoholic drinks. The shop shown here later became a post office.

A group of older gentlemen outside the Queen Anne public house on Junction Road, Deane, opposite Deane Church, c. 1905. Since there are ten of them it is likely that they have had 'breakfast' (usually beer) before setting off on a bowling 'picnic', which was usually more beer.

Civic Pride. The Mayor of Bolton Council, Alderman Thomas Fletcher, on the steps of The Pike, with the house's owner John Heywood (the only clean-shaven gentlemen) behind, 27 August 1887. This is the luncheon party just before the stone-laying for High Street Branch Library on land given by Heywood. To the right of the Mayor is Town Clerk R.E. Hinnell, to his left J.K. Waite, the Chief Librarian. The house name is marked by the Pike View Hotel, Derby Street – not so named because Rivington Pike can be seen from it, as is often stated.

Trainspotters at Crescent Road engine sheds, late 1950s. A very keen group of Cub Scouts note down the number of the loco at the large engine sheds at Crescent Road, built in the mid-1870s. The sheds serviced steam locomotives until 1968 and were demolished the following year. The area is now a housing estate although the Bolton to Manchester line is still nearby.

An advertising coupon for Charles Willis, an enterprising and early Bolton photographer who went on to be the official photographer for the Borough. His studios in Newport Street were among the first to use strong electric light, which reduced exposure times and gave a clearer image. Much of his early work was turned into very popular local postcards. A 'cabinet' photograph was 6¼ in deep by 4½ in and mounted on strong board for display.

FURTHER READING

Barton, B.T., *Historical Gleanings*
Baines, E., *History of Lancashire*
Brimelow, W., *The Political and Parliamentary History of Bolton*
Clegg, James, *Annals of Bolton*
Gent, Leslie, *Bolton Past* (1995)
Hamer, H., *Bolton 1838–1938*
Hamer, H. and Sparke, A., *The Book of Bolton* (1929)
Longworth, James, *Cotton Mills of Bolton, 1780–1985*
Readyhough, Gordon, *Bolton Town Centre, A Modern History (Parts 1 & 2)*
Readyhough, Gordon, *Pubs of Bolton Town Centre (1986)*
Scholes, J.C., *History of Bolton*
Victoria County History of Lancashire
Plus the many and varied publications by Neil Richardson, 375 Chorley Road, Swinton.

Most of these books are still available in local bookshops and at 'Artefacts' in the main library foyer. Others may be consulted in the Local History Library.